AAX-3926

M.AC
D35
M372
Gr. 9-12

Math Connections
High School Activites · Blackline Masters

David J. Glatzer and Joyce Glat

D0808629

Algebra
Reasoning
Geometry
Communication
Precalculus
Problem Solving

7552

DALE SEYMOUR PUBLICATIONS

BELMONT UNIVERSITY LIBRARY
CURRICULUM LAB

Managing Editor: Michael Kane
Project Editor: Joan Gideon
Production Manager: Janet Yearian
Production Coordinator: Leanne Collins
Design Manager: Jeff Kelly
Text Design: Lisa Raine

This book is published by Dale Seymour Publications, an imprint of the Alternative Publishing Group of Addison-Wesley.

Copyright © 1993 by Dale Seymour Publications. All rights reserved. Printed in the United States of America.

Limited reproduction permission. The publisher grants permission to individual teachers who have purchased this book to reproduce the blackline masters as needed for use with their own students. Reproduction for an entire school or school district or for commercial use is prohibited.

ISBN 0-86651-633-6
Order number DS21204
12 3 4 5 6 7-MA-97 96 95 94 93 92

DALE
SEYMOUR
PUBLICATIONS
P.O. Box 10888
Palo Alto, CA. 94303

This book is printed
on recycled paper.

Contents

Introduction

Purpose

The purpose of the blackline masters in *Math Connection: High School Activities* is to offer secondary mathematics teachers (grades 9–12) a variety of non-routine problem activities, designed to foster the development of critical thinking skills while reinforcing concepts from the mathematics curriculum. The activities ask students to verbalize understanding and to contrast major mathematical ideas. The book is a sequel to two similar volumes also published by Dale Seymour Publications, *Math Connections* (1989) and *Math Intersections* (1990), written by the same authors for use with middle grade students (grades 6–9).

Philosophy

As specified in the NCTM's *Curriculum and Evaluation Standards for School Mathematics* (1989), activities at the secondary level should encourage communication, reasoning, and problem solving. The non-routine activities in this book do just that. Each different type of activity addresses higher levels of thinking and encourages both good reasoning and communication of students' ideas about how mathematics works. As students use the activities in this book, they will begin functioning at higher levels of thinking and will increase their confidence in their ability to discuss mathematics. Through these activities, students can develop a sense of their own "mathematical power."

Organization

The book is organized in six sections, each with a different activity format. The first five sections draw on concepts presented in elementary algebra, intermediate algebra, geometry, and pre-calculus, with two pages of problems per section based on each of these secondary level courses. The final section, "Making the Connection," contains a variety of activity formats, each page dealing with concepts from both algebra and geometry. The problems are arranged in order of difficulty.

The introduction to each section explains the nature of that section's activity, works through sample problems, and describes the follow-up or COMPLETING THE CONNECTION questions typical of that section. These questions, found at the end of each page, are intended to help you assess the students' overall understanding and help them reach closure.

Suggested answers are provided in the Answer Section of this book, although for many problems, students may come up with other acceptable solutions or rationales. As a model, the first problem on each page is answered for the student.

Use of the Material

There is no one way to use this book. It can be adapted to the needs of your students. However, they will receive the greatest benefit if you provide opportunities for them to share the thought processes they used in arriving at their answers.

- *Classroom discussion.* Make a photocopy of the page for each student and a transparency of the same page for yourself. Discuss the problems one at a time, encouraging the students to support their answers.

- *Small-group work.* Divide the students into small groups (of, say, three or four each), and have each group thoroughly discuss each problem. This approach may follow the model of cooperative learning groups.
- *Share with a neighbor.* Ask the students to complete the page independently and then share their responses with a partner.
- *Student-generated extensions.* When the class finishes a page, ask the students to write additional problems in the same form. These should also be shared with other students.

Conclusion

Remember that the activities in this book:

- Can be used to provide variety in the math curriculum.
- Can be used to preview and review
- Can be used to increase student involvement
- Are easily adaptable
- Are open-ended and easily extended
- Are fun

The ideas contained in this book have been used successfully in classrooms at the secondary level.

Section One
How Do You Know That?

Introduction

The *How Do You Know That?* activity provides an opportunity for the students to use words to express key concepts in mathematics. The ability to explain relationships is a better indicator of comprehension than the mechanical manipulation of symbols found in standard exercises. Therefore, the focus of this activity is relationships rather than manipulation. Cooperative learning and divergent thinking are encouraged.

For each question in this section, the student is asked to write one or more complete sentences. Responses will vary. In formulating responses, the students should use their knowledge of definitions, relationships, and properties.

Sample Exercises

Write one or more complete sentences to answer each question. Answers may vary.

1. How do you know that the graph of $x^2 + 4y^2 = 36$ is not a circle?

   In order to make a circle, the coefficient of the x^2 and y^2 terms must be the same.

2. How do you know that 8, 8, and 18 cannot be the lengths of the sides of a triangle?

   In a triangle, the sum of the lengths of any two sides must be greater than the length of the third side. $8 + 8 < 18$.

COMPLETING THE CONNECTION

To summarize this activity, the *Completing the Connection* question asks the students to reflect on the concepts they used to answer the "How do you know that . . ." questions. Specifically, they are asked to identify one concept used for each page. For example, on the "Elementary Algebra" pages, a student might respond with the concept of "slope" or the concept of "what it means for a point to be on a line." Answers will vary. Students should share their responses to increase recognition of concepts and properties.

Write one or more complete sentences to answer each question. Answers may vary.

1. How do you know that $(3, 5)$ is not on the line $2x + 3y = 6$?

   Since $2(3) + 3(5) \neq 6$, the point $(3, 5)$ is not on the line.

2. How do you know that $5x$ is not the greatest common factor of $-30x^3y$, $20x^4$, and $50x^2y^5$?

3. How do you know that the product of an odd number of negative numbers is a negative number?

4. How do you know that the following is not the graph of $y = \dfrac{1}{2}x + 2$?

5. How do you know that $\dfrac{x^2 + y^2}{(x + y)^2}$ does not simplify to 1?

6. How do you know that $-16 = m^2$ has no real solutions?

7. How do you know that the y-intercept of the line represented by the equation $3x - 4y = 8$ is -2?

8. How do you know that $x^2 + 9$ is non-factorable over the set of real numbers?

COMPLETING THE CONNECTION
Identify one concept that you used to answer a question on this page.

Write one or more complete sentences to answer each question. Answers may vary.

1. How do you know that $4^3 = 2^6$?

   Since $4^3 = 4 \times 4 \times 4$ and $2^6 = 2 \times 2 \times 2 \times 2 \times 2 \times 2$ by grouping pairs of two's $(2 \times 2)(2 \times 2)(2 \times 2)$, it is clear that $4^3 = 2^6$.

2. How do you know that the value of x that satisfies the equation $4x = 30$ is not an integer?

3. How do you know that $\dfrac{x-a}{a-x} = -1$, where $(x \neq a)$?

4. How do you know that $(a + b)^2 \neq a^2 + b^2$?

5. How do you know that $(2x - 1)$ is a factor of $2x^2 - 17x + 8$?

6. How do you know that if $(x - 4)(x - 5)(x - 6) = 0$, x cannot be 7?

7. How do you know that the lines represented by the equations $3x = y$ and $y - 3x = 1$ are parallel?

8. How do you know that the points $(4, 7)$, $(-1, -8)$, and $(0, -5)$ lie on a straight line?

COMPLETING THE CONNECTION
Identify one concept that you used to answer a question on this page.

Write one or more complete sentences to answer each question. Answers may vary.

1. How do you know that $x^2 + y^2 = 36$ is not a function?

   The graph of the equation is a circle, and a circle cannot be a function because of the vertical line test.

2. How do you know that the graph of $y = |x|$ is symmetric about the y-axis?

3. How do you know that the lines represented by the equations $2x - 3y = 6$ and $4x - 6y = 9$ are parallel?

4. How do you know that the equation $x^2 - 8 = 0$ has irrational roots?

5. How do you know that $(x - 2)$ is not a factor of $x^3 - 3x^2 + 14x - 20$?

6. How do you know that the graph of the equation $x^2 + 2x + 2y^2 + 1 = 0$ is not a circle?

7. How do you know that 6, 12, 24, 48, . . . is a geometric sequence?

8. How do you know that $\log_b xy = \log_b x + \log_b y$?

COMPLETING THE CONNECTION
Identify one concept that you used to answer a question on this page.

Write one or more complete sentences to answer each question. Answers may vary.

1. How do you know that $|a + b| \neq |a| + |b|$?

   If $a = 5$ and $b = -10$, $|a + b| = |-5| = 5$ and $|a| + |b| = |5| + |-10| = 15$.

2. How do you know that the product $(a + bi)(a - bi)$ is a real number?

3. How do you know that $y = x^2$ and $y = x^2 - 4x + 4$ are translations of each other?

4. How do you know that the graph of the equation $x^2 - 4y^2 - 6x = 7$ is a hyperbola?

5. How do you know that the equation $4^x = 25$ cannot be solved without a calculator or tables?

6. How do you know that $h(x) = -\left(\dfrac{1}{2}\right)^x$ is an increasing function?

7. How do you know that $\dfrac{2}{3}$ is not a root of $8x^3 - 5x^2 + 6x + 4 = 0$?

8. How do you know that $f(x) = 2x + 2$ and $g(x) = \dfrac{1}{2}x - 1$ are inverse functions?

COMPLETING THE CONNECTION
Identify one concept that you used to answer a question on this page.

Write one or more complete sentences to answer each question. Answers may vary.

1. How do you know that all equilateral triangles are similar?

   Each angle of an equilateral triangle measures 60°. Therefore, all equilateral triangles have the same shape.

2. How do you know that the lengths 5, 6, and 7 do not represent a Pythagorean triple?

3. How do you know that a triangle cannot have sides with lengths of 10, 10, and 25?

4. How do you know that Angle-Angle-Angle would not be a method of establishing that two triangles are congruent?

5. How do you know that a triangle inscribed in a semicircle must be a right triangle?

6. How do you know that the midpoints of all congruent chords of a circle form another circle concentric with the given circle?

7. How do you know that a square is the only regular polygon in which the measure of each interior angle is the same as the measure of each exterior angle?

8. How do you know that 1900° cannot be the sum of the measures of the interior angles of a convex polygon?

COMPLETING THE CONNECTION
Identify one concept that you used to answer a question on this page.

Write one or more complete sentences to answer each question. Answers may vary.

1. How do you know that a right triangle cannot be similar to an obtuse triangle?

    Similar triangles must have congruent corresponding angles. The right angle will not be congruent to the obtuse angle.

2. How do you know that all squares are similar?

3. How do you know that the exterior angles at the base of an isosceles triangle are congruent?

4. How do you know that a triangle with sides 5, 6, and 10 is obtuse?

5. How do you know that the points with coordinates (0, 0), (0, 4), (8, 0), and (11, 4) cannot be the vertices of a parallelogram?

6. How do you know that the points with coordinates (4, 5), (7, 7), and (10, 9) would be collinear?

7. How do you know that the diagonals of a non-square rectangle are not perpendicular?

8. How do you know that if two lines are parallel, the bisectors of the interior angles on the same side of the transversal form a right angle?

COMPLETING THE CONNECTION
Identify one concept that you used to answer a question on this page.

Write one or more complete sentences to answer each question. Answers may vary.

1. How do you know that the tan 90° is undefined?

    $$\tan 90° = \frac{\sin 90°}{\cos 90°} = \frac{1}{0} \text{ which is undefined.}$$

2. How do you know that the period of $y = 2\cos\frac{1}{2}x$ is 4π?

3. How do you know that you don't need trig tables or a calculator to find sin 330°?

4. How do you know that 2 is the maximum value of $4 \sin x \cos x$?

5. How do you know that a cubic equation with real coefficients must have at least one real root?

6. How do you know that $y = \frac{1}{x^2 - 36}$ has exactly two vertical asymptotes?

7. How do you know that $\log_2 25$ is between 4 and 5?

8. How do you know that $x^2 + y^2 = 2$ has an area twice as great as $x^2 + y^2 = 1$?

COMPLETING THE CONNECTION
Identify one concept that you used to answer a question on this page.

Write one or more complete sentences to answer each question. Answers may vary.

1. How do you know that $\sin^2 x + \cos^2 x$ will never equal 2?

   $\sin^2 x + \cos^2 x = 1$ is an identity. Therefore it always has a value of 1 and cannot have any different value.

2. How do you know that $y = \sin x$ is periodic?

3. How do you know that $\sin 60° > \sin 1$ radian?

4. How do you know that 11, 101, 1001, 10001, . . . is neither an arithmetic nor a geometric sequence?

5. How do you know that $\dfrac{1}{2} + \dfrac{1}{4} + \dfrac{1}{8} + . . .$ converges and $\dfrac{1}{2} + \dfrac{1}{3} + \dfrac{1}{4} + . . .$ diverges?

6. How do you know that a cubic equation with real coefficients cannot have roots -1, -3, and $2 - i$?

7. How do you know that the sum of the numerical coefficients in $(x + y)^5$ is 32?

8. How do you know that the Pythagorean Theorem is a special case of the Law of Cosines?

COMPLETING THE CONNECTION
Identify one concept that you used to answer a question on this page.

Introduction

The *Sometimes* activity asks students to focus on a given condition that is true in some cases and not in others. If the activity had a standard true/false format, each given statement would have to be classified as false, because there is always a counterexample. It is important for students to understand that in order for a statement to be true, it must be true under *all* conditions. This activity format is more effective than standard *true/false* or *sometimes/ always/never* questions because it does not allow students to guess. For each condition, they are asked to provide one example in which the condition is true and one example in which it is false.

Sample Exercises

Each condition given below is true in some cases and false in at least one instance. For each numbered item, give one example that shows when the condition is true and one that shows when it is false. Your answer may take the form of a diagram, an equation, a numerical or variable expression, or a written response.

Condition	True	False
1. $x^2 - k$ is factorable.	$x^2 - 9$	$x^2 - 8$
2. The exterior angles of a regular polygon are acute.	regular hexagon — exterior angle measures 60°.	equilateral triangle — exterior angle measures 120°.

COMPLETING THE CONNECTION

To conclude each page, the students are asked in the *Completing the Connection* question to generate any statement, based on content within the relevant subject area, that is true *all* the time. These statements are likely to be definitions, properties, or theorems. For example, on the "Elementary Algebra" pages, a student might offer the identity "$(a^2 - b^2) = (a + b)(a - b)$."

Each condition given below is true in some cases and false in at least one instance. For each numbered item, give one example that shows when the condition is true and one that shows when it is false. Your answer may take the form of a diagram, an expression, an equation, or a written response.

Condition	True	False
1. $(-1)^n$ is negative.	$(-1)^5 = 1$	$(-1)^6 = +1$
2. $x^2 = 2x$		
3. If $p < q$, then $pr < qr$.		
4. The lines represented by the two equations are parallel: $2x + 4y = 9$ $4x + ky = 16$		
5. $(a + b)^2 = a^2 + b^2$		
6. $x^2 + kx - 6$ is factorable.		
7. $\sqrt{a} < \sqrt{a^3}$		
8. If x represents some number between $\frac{2}{3}$ and $\frac{3}{2}$, then $3x > 3$.		

COMPLETING THE CONNECTION
Write a statement from elementary algebra that is always true.
Be prepared to justify your response.

Each condition given below is true in some cases and false in at least one instance. For each numbered item, give one example that shows when the condition is true and one that shows when it is false. Your answer may take the form of a diagram, an expression, an equation, or a written response.

Condition	True	False
1. $\lvert a \rvert = a$	$\lvert 6 \rvert = 6$	$\lvert {}^{-}8 \rvert \neq {}^{-}8$
2. If $a^2 = b^2$, then $a = b$.		
3. $x^2 > 1$		
4. $x^y = y^x$ for whole numbers x and y.		
5. $\sqrt{a+b} = \sqrt{a} + \sqrt{b}$		
6. $ax^2 + bx + c$ is a square trinomial.		
7. The graph of $y = 3x + b$ passes through quadrants 1, 2, and 3.		
8. For two ordered pairs, the slope of the line through the points is less than 0.		

COMPLETING THE CONNECTION

Write a statement from elementary algebra that is always true.
Be prepared to justify your response.

Each condition given below is true in some cases and false in at least one instance. For each numbered item, give one example that shows when the condition is true and one that shows when it is false. Your answer may take the form of a diagram, an expression, an equation, or a written response.

Condition	True	False
1. $4x^2 + kx + 1$ is factorable.	$4x^2 + 4x + 1 = (2x + 1)^2$	$4x^2 + 3x + 1$ is prime
2. $\sqrt{x^2}$ is a real number.		
3. The point $(5, k)$ is on the circle represented by the equation $x^2 + y^2 = 25$.		
4. The product of two complex numbers is real.		
5. The graphs of $x = k$ and $x^2 + y^2 = 100$ intersect in exactly two points.		
6. Two lines with the same slope are parallel.		
7. All linear relations are functions.		
8. $f(g(x)) = g(f(x))$		

COMPLETING THE CONNECTION
Write a statement from intermediate algebra that is always true.
Be prepared to justify your response.

Each condition given below is true in some cases and false in at least one instance. For each numbered item, give one example that shows when the condition is true and one that shows when it is false. Your answer may take the form of a diagram, an expression, an equation, or a written response.

Condition	True	False
1. $\dfrac{2-x}{x-2} = -1$	$\dfrac{2-7}{7-2} = -1$	$\dfrac{2-2}{2-2}$ is indeterminate
2. The sum of two irrational numbers is irrational.		
3. Two lines that are perpendicular have slopes that are negative reciprocals of each other.		
4. $\sqrt[k]{x}$ is defined for all real values of x.		
5. The equation of a hyperbola contains x^2.		
6. $i^k = 1$		
7. A function has an inverse.		
8. $(a + b)^3 = a^3 + b^3$		

COMPLETING THE CONNECTION
Write a statement from intermediate algebra that is always true.
Be prepared to justify your response.

Each condition given below is true in some cases and false in at least one instance. For each numbered item, give one example that shows when the condition is true and one that shows when it is false. Your answer may take the form of a diagram, an expression, an equation, or a written response.

Condition	True	False
1. A parallelogram whose diagonals are congruent is a square.		
2. A median of a triangle divides the triangle into two congruent triangles.		
3. The shortest side of a right triangle is half the hypotenuse.		
4. The volume of a cylinder with height 5" is greater than the volume of a cone with height 5".		
5. In a triangle, the altitude and the median are the same line segment.		
6. The locus of points four units from a given circle is one circle.		
7. Two circles will have exactly four common tangents.		
8. A figure that has line symmetry has rotational symmetry.		

COMPLETING THE CONNECTION
Write a statement from geometry that is always true.
Be prepared to justify your response.

Each condition given below is true in some cases and false in at least one instance. For each numbered item, give one example that shows when the condition is true and one that shows when it is false. Your answer may take the form of a diagram, an expression, an equation, or a written response.

Condition	True	False
1. Right triangles are similar to each other.		
2. Three points are collinear.		
3. The two smallest angles of a triangle are complementary.		
4. Rectangles have perpendicular diagonals.		
5. The figure formed by joining the midpoints of the sides of a parallelogram is a rectangle.		
6. The exterior angles of a regular polygon are obtuse.		
7. A transformation preserves the distance between two points.		
8. A line perpendicular to a chord of a circle bisects the chord.		

COMPLETING THE CONNECTION
Write a statement from geometry that is always true.
Be prepared to justify your response.

Each condition given below is true in some cases and false in at least one instance. For each numbered item, give one example that shows when the condition is true and one that shows when it is false. Your answer may take the form of a diagram, an expression, an equation, or a written response.

Condition	True	False
1. $\sin x = \cos x$	$\sin 45° = \cos 45°$	$\sin 30° \neq \cos 30°$
2. $y = \dfrac{1}{x^2 - k}$ will have two vertical asymptotes.		
3. A cubic equation with real coefficients will have three real roots.		
4. An absolute value function is symmetric with respect to the y-axis.		
5. The point $(5, 4)$ is inside the circle represented by the equation $x^2 + y^2 = r^2$.		
6. A geometric series with a first term a and a common ratio r converges.		
7. $f(x) = (x - 1)^r$, r being an integer greater than 1; $f(x)$ is an increasing function.		
8. For a given function, there is an inverse function.		

COMPLETING THE CONNECTION
Write a statement from pre-calculus that is always true.
Be prepared to justify your response.

Each condition given below is true in some cases and false in at least one instance. For each numbered item, give one example that shows when the condition is true and one that shows when it is false. Your answer may take the form of a diagram, an expression, an equation, or a written response.

Condition	True	False
1. $\sin x + \cos x < 1$	If $x = 180°$, $\sin 180° + \cos 180° = 0 + (-1) = -1 < 1$	If $x = 45°$, $\sin 45° + \cos 45° + \cos 45° = \dfrac{\sqrt{2}}{2} + \dfrac{\sqrt{2}}{2} = \sqrt{2} \nless 1$
2. A fourth-degree equation with real coefficients will have four real roots.		
3. $(4, 0)$, $(7, 2)$, and $(10, k)$ are collinear.		
4. $\tan(\alpha + \beta) = \tan\alpha + \tan\beta$		
5. $y = x^r$, r being an integer, is symmetric with respect to the origin.		
6. One can find $\log_2 k$ without a calculator.		
7. $y = k$ is tangent to the ellipse $x^2 + 4y^2 = 36$.		
8. If $P(x)$ is a polynomial with real coefficients, then P has at least one real zero.		

COMPLETING THE CONNECTION

Write a statement from pre-calculus that is always true.

Be prepared to justify your response.

Section Three
What If?

Introduction

In the *What If?* activity, students explore the impact of specific conditions of a situation or of changes in those conditions. They are asked to determine what will happen as certain indicated changes are made. This activity fosters the development of reasoning skills.

For each question in this section, the students are asked to write one or more complete sentences. Encourage them, as they formulate their responses, to examine specific examples that fit the condition and to use drawings or manipulatives to help them visualize the situation.

Sample Exercises

Write one or more complete sentences to answer each question.

1. What happens to the value of the expression $\dfrac{3}{1-m}$ if $m > 1$?

   The value of the expression will be less than 0.

2. What are the coordinates of the endpoint of a segment if the other endpoint is (–4, 3) and the midpoint of the segment is (2, 1)?

   The x-coordinate of the midpoint is the average of the x-coordinates of the endpoints. Thus $\dfrac{x+(-4)}{2} = 2$ and $x = 8$. Similarly for the y-coordinate $\dfrac{y+3}{2} = 1$ and $y = -1$. The endpoint is (8, –1).

COMPLETING THE CONNECTION

As a follow-up, *Completing the Connection* asks students to select a mathematical word found on the page and write or illustrate its definition. On a "Geometry" page, for example, a student might select the word *complementary* and give the definition "two angles whose sum totals 90°."

Write one or more complete sentences to answer each question.

1. What happens to the solution of the equation $ax + b = c$ if you triple both sides of the equation?

   Nothing happens to the solution, because you can then divide both sides of the equation by 3.

2. What can you say about the point with coordinates $(6, 4)$ if you know that the point with coordinates $(5, 4)$ is on the line $y = x - 1$?

3. What happens to the graph of the line $y = 4x + k$ if k increases?

4. What happens to the slope of the line of $Ax + By = C$ if $A > 0$ and $B < 0$?

5. What does the graph of a system of linear equations look like if the product of the slopes of the lines is -1?

6. What happens to the value of $\dfrac{7}{k - 5}$ if $k < 5$?

7. What happens to the point on a graph if you add 2 to each number in the ordered pair?

8. What can be said about the expression $x^2 - by^2$ if $\sqrt{b}$ is an integer?

COMPLETING THE CONNECTION
Select a mathematical term found on this page and write or illustrate the definition of the term.

Write one or more complete sentences to answer each question.

1. What will happen to the value of a number x if the number is squared?

   If x is negative or greater than 1, the value will be larger. However, when you square a number $0 < x < 1$, the value will be smaller. If $x = 1$, the value stays the same.

2. What will happen to the inequality $x < 2$ if both sides of the inequality are multiplied by -1?

3. What happens to the absolute value of an expression if you take the opposite of the quantity before taking the absolute value?

4. What happens to the value of the expression $\sqrt{x}$ if the value of x is doubled?

5. What happens to the value of the expression $\dfrac{x+a}{x-b}$ if $x = b$?

6. What happens to the consecutive even integers x, $x + 2$, $x + 4$ if you add x to each integer?

7. What happens to the slope of the line represented by the equation $y = mx + b$ if m is doubled?

8. What happens to the solution of the following system of equations if $a = d$, $b = e$, and $c \neq f$?

   $$ax + by = c$$
   $$dx + ey = f$$

COMPLETING THE CONNECTION

Select a mathematical term found on this page and write or illustrate the definition of the term.

Write one or more complete sentences to answer each question.

1. What happens to the graph of the parabola $y = x^2 + h$ if h increases?

   The parabola moves "up" as h increases.

2. What happens to the value of i^n if n is even?

3. What can you say about the point $(0, 3)$ if you know that the point $(0, 5)$ is on a circle centered at the origin?

4. What happens to the nature of the roots of $3x^2 + kx + 3 = 0$ if $k > 6$ or $k < -6$?

5. What happens to the graph of the equation $y = a^x$ if a is between 0 and 1 and x increases?

6. What happens to the sum of the series $a + ar + ar^2 + \ldots$ if $|r| < 1$?

7. What happens to x with respect to y, v, and w, if w varies jointly as x and the square of y, and inversely as v?

8. What happens to the graph of the line $y = -x + b$ and the graph of the hyperbola $xy = 1$ if b has a value of 2 or -2?

COMPLETING THE CONNECTION

Select a mathematical term found on this page and write or illustrate the definition of the term.

Write one or more complete sentences to answer each question.

1. What happens to the value of $f(x) = x^2 + 2x$ if the value of x is tripled?

   There is no consistent answer. The change will vary with different values for x.

2. What results if you join the coordinates of the midpoints of consecutive sides of a quadrilateral with vertices at $(1, 3)$, $(1, 7)$, $(7, 3)$, and $(7, 7)$?

3. What happens to the graph of $y = ax^2 + bx + c$ if $a < 0$?

4. What happens to the nature of the roots of $ax^2 + bx + c = 0$ if $b^2 - 4ac < 0$?

5. What happens to the sum of the series $a + ar + ar^2 + \ldots$ if $|r| > 2$?

6. What happens to the sum of an arithmetic series if each term is doubled?

7. Given that x varies inversely as the square of y, what happens to the value of y if the value of x is doubled?

8. What is the relationship between $f(x) = ax + b$ and its inverse function if $a = 1$ and $b = 0$?

COMPLETING THE CONNECTION

Select a mathematical term found on this page and write or illustrate the definition of the term.

Write one or more complete sentences to answer each question.

1. What happens to a triangle whose base is at $(0, 0)$ and $(3, 0)$ if the other vertex is moved from $(0, 4)$ to $(1.5, 4)$?

   The triangle changes from a right triangle to one that is not a right triangle. However the area stays the same.

2. What happens to the slope of a line segment connecting the points $(0, 0)$ and (a, b) if the values of a and b are doubled?

3. What happens to the distance of the point $(5, 12)$ from the origin if the point is reflected over the *x*-axis?

4. What results if you connect the midpoints of all congruent chords in a circle with radius 7"?

5. What happens to the area of a rectangle whose coordinates are $A(1, 2)$, $B(5, 2)$, $C(1, 4)$, and $D(5, 4)$ if point B is moved to $(10, 2)$ and point D is moved to $(10, 4)$?

6. What happens to the length of the median of a trapezoid if each base is doubled?

7. What happens to the measure of the arc *AC* if $m\angle B$ is halved?

8. What happens to the volume of a cylinder if the radius is doubled and the height is doubled?

COMPLETING THE CONNECTION
Select a mathematical term found on this page and write or illustrate the definition of the term.

Write one or more complete sentences to answer each question.

1. What results if you take the complement of the complement of an angle?

   You get back to the original angle.

2. What happens to the area of a triangle if you double the base and cut the altitude in half?

3. What happens to the hypotenuse of a right triangle if you double the length of the legs of the triangle?

4. What happens to the length of the sides of the larger of two similar triangles in the ratio of 1:2 if you add 5 to the length of each side of the smaller triangle?

5. What happens to the area of a sector of a circle if you double the measure of the central angle and double the measure of the radius?

6. What happens to the volume of a sphere if you triple the radius?

7. What results if you connect the midpoints of the consecutive sides of a rectangle?

8. What happens to the sum of the measures of the interior angles of a regular polygon if the number of sides of the polygon is increased by four?

COMPLETING THE CONNECTION

Select a mathematical term found on this page and write or illustrate the definition of the term.

Write one or more complete sentences to answer each question.

1. What happens to the graph of $y = \cos x$ if the period is cut in half?

   If you cut the period in half (from 2π to π), an entire period of cosine results from 0 to π.

2. What results if you take the reciprocals of the terms in a geometric sequence?

3. Given that the equation $x^2 + y^2 = 9$ represents a circle, what happens to the equation if the center of the circle is moved to $(8, 0)$?

4. What happens to the graph of $xy = 1$ if you take the absolute value of the left side of the equation?

5. What happens to the area of a triangle with sides a and b if the measure of the angle between a and b gets larger?

6. What happens to the symmetry of the graph of $2y = x^r$ if r changes from an even to an odd integer?

7. What happens to the graph of $\dfrac{y^2}{a^2} - \dfrac{x^2}{b^2} = 1$ if $a = b$?

8. What happens to the graph of the equation $r = a \cos n\,\theta$ if n is odd?

COMPLETING THE CONNECTION

Select a mathematical term found on this page and write or illustrate the definition of the term.

Write one or more complete sentences to answer each question.

1. What happens to the equation if the graph of $y = 2(x + 3)^2 - 2$ is translated to the right four units?

   Since $y = (x - 4)^2$ is four units to the right of $y = x^2$, the new equation would be $y = 2(x - 1)^2 - 2$.

2. What happens to the graph of $y = \sin x$ if the period is tripled?

3. What happens to an infinite geometric series if $|r| < 1$?

4. What happens to an arithmetic sequence if 6 is added to each term in the sequence?

5. What happens to the graph of $y = \sin x$ if you take the absolute value of right side of the equation?

6. What would you say about the type of function you had if, for the function f, there exists a positive real number p such that $f(x + p) = f(x)$?

7. What happens to the sum of the coefficients of $(x + y)^r$ if r is doubled (r being a positive integer)?

8. What will the population of a city be at the end of 35 years if it has a population of 40,000 and the population increases 10% every 5 years?

COMPLETING THE CONNECTION

Select a mathematical term found on this page and write or illustrate the definition of the term.

Introduction

In the *Example to Fit the Condition* activity, students demonstrate their understanding of basic mathematical concepts and relationships. For a given condition, they are asked to list, write, draw, find, or show one or more specified examples that fit the condition. Because the activity is open-ended, student responses will vary. All ideas should be shared in a group discussion, during which other students make certain that each response does in fact fit the condition. As responses are shared, encourage students to communicate the properties and attributes that are critical for the question at hand.

Sample Exercises

For the given condition, provide example(s) as directed.

1. List three sets of measures that represent the lengths of sides of a triangle.

   $6, 6, 6$
   $3, 4, 5$
   $2, 2, 3$

2. Write a system of two linear equations that represent parallel lines

   $x + 2y = 4$
   $x + 2y = 7$

Of course, other answers are possible for both of the above sample questions.

COMPLETING THE CONNECTION

In *Completing the Connection,* students are asked to state the concept illustrated by a "visual definition." For example, given the following illustration, geometry students would be expected to indicate that the picture represents the definition of a central angle of a circle.

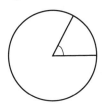

31

For each statement, provide an example, diagram, number, expression, equation, or written response to meet the given condition.

1. Write the equation of a line parallel to the line $2x + 4y = 6$.

   $6x + 12y = 10$

2. List the coordinates of four points, each 10 units from the origin.

3. Write two monomials whose product is $-18x^3y^4$.

4. Write a trinomial that has $2x + 3$ as one of its factors.

5. Write a quadratic equation whose roots are $x = 3$, $x = -2$.

6. Write a quadratic equation that contains a perfect square trinomial.

7. Write the equation for two lines that intersect at the point $(1, 1)$.

8. Write a rational expression which cannot be simplified and which contains a numerator and denominator that are each binomials.

COMPLETING THE CONNECTION

Identify the concept or relationship represented by the given illustration.

$$a^2 - b^2 = (a + b)(a - b)$$

For each statement, provide an example, diagram, number, expression, equation, or written response to meet the given condition.

1. List two radical expressions whose product is between 6 and 7.

   $\sqrt{8}$ $\sqrt{5}$

2. Write two exponential expressions, each having a base of b, that have a quotient of b.

3. List any three points contained on a line having slope $-\dfrac{2}{3}$.

4. Draw on a number line the graph of $|x| \leq 4$.

5. Write three irrational numbers, each with a value less than 5.

6. Write an equation that has exactly three solutions.

7. Write an algebraic identity corresponding to the following diagram.

	x	y
x	x^2	xy
y	xy	y^2

8. Write an algebraic expression that shows b has been increased by 10%.

COMPLETING THE CONNECTION

Identify the concept or relationship represented by the given illustration.

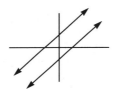

For each statement, provide an example, diagram, number, expression, equation, or written response to meet the given condition.

1. Write the equation for a circle formed by moving the circle $x^2 + y^2 = 16$ five units horizontally and four units vertically.

   $(x - 5)^2 + (y - 4)^2 = 16$

2. Write the equations for four circles, each tangent to the line $x = 7$.

3. Write an equation with real coefficients that has $1 + i$ as a root.

4. Write an arithmetic series of five terms whose sum is 30.

5. Write a binomial raised to a power which, when expanded, has a second term of $12x^2y$.

6. Write two functions that are inverses of each other.

7. State the coordinates of the vertices of any equilateral triangle.

8. Write a problem involving some physical phenomenon that illustrates inverse variation.

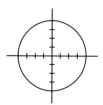

COMPLETING THE CONNECTION

Identify the concept or relationship represented by the given illustration.

For each statement, provide an example, diagram, number, expression, equation, or written response to meet the given condition.

1. Draw a concave parabola, opening upward, symmetric about the line $x = 2$, with its vertex on the x-axis.

2. Write two equations: one for a circle centered at the origin, and one for a line tangent to the circle.

3. Write two equations: one for a circle centered at the origin, and one for a parabola intersecting the circle in exactly three points.

4. Write an exponential equation indicating that a certain power of 2 is equal to a different power of 4.

5. State an absolute value inequality whose solution would be all points on the number line between –3 and 4 inclusive.

6. Write an arithmetic sequence with 8 as the third term and a common difference of 5.

7. Write an equation given that the highest degree is 3 and two roots of the equation are $5i$ and –1.

8. State a formula illustrating direct variation.

COMPLETING THE CONNECTION

Identify the concept or relationship represented by the given illustration.

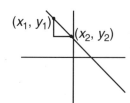

For each statement, provide a diagram or numbers to meet the given condition.

1. Draw an isosceles trapezoid in which the shorter base is congruent to the legs.

2. Draw a square formed by connecting the midpoints of the sides of a special quadrilateral.

3. Draw a parallelogram with diagonals that are perpendicular and congruent.

4. Draw a diagram showing two adjacent supplementary angles whose measures are in the ratio 2:1.

5. List the measures of two different rectangular pyramids, each with a volume of 12 cubic units.

6. Draw a non-rectangular parallelogram situated in the first quadrant of a coordinate grid and having a base of 10 units and an area of 50 square units.

7. Draw two rhombuses, each with a perimeter of 40 cm, one having an area close to 100 and one having an area under 10.

8. Draw a circle formed by connecting the midpoints of congruent chords within another circle.

COMPLETING THE CONNECTION
Identify the concept or relationship represented by the given illustration.

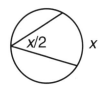

For each statement, provide a diagram to meet the given condition.

1. Draw a right scalene triangle.

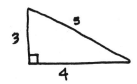

2. Draw an isosceles obtuse triangle.

3. Draw a triangle with three lines of symmetry.

4. Draw a pair of similar triangles with a ratio of similitude 2:3.

5. Draw a regular polygon with an exterior angle of 60°.

6. Draw two circles having two common external tangents.

7. Draw a parallelogram with diagonals that are perpendicular.

8. Draw a quadrilateral with line symmetry and rotational symmetry.

COMPLETING THE CONNECTION
Identify the concept or relationship represented by the given illustration.

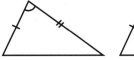

For each statement, provide an example, diagram, number, expression, equation, or written response to meet the given condition.

1. Show a trigonometric function having a range between −1 and 1, inclusive.

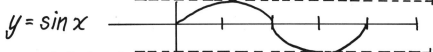

$y = \sin x$

2. Show a periodic function that is not trigonometric.

3. Write the equation for a circle tangent to both axes, with its center in the first quadrant and an area equal to 9π square units.

4. List three different degree measures in the third quadrant such that you could find $\cos \theta$ without the use of a calculator.

5. Write a formula, involving the sine function, for the area of a triangle.

6. Write the polar coordinates represented by the rectangular coordinates $1 + i$.

7. Write an equation for an ellipse tangent to both axes and with its center at (−5, −6).

8. Write an infinite geometric series having a limit of 2 for its sum.

COMPLETING THE CONNECTION

Identify the concept or relationship represented in the given illustration.

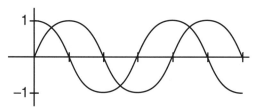

For each statement, provide an example, diagram, number, expression, equation, or written response to meet the given condition.

1. Write a trigonometric identity illustrated by the following diagram.

$sin^2 \theta + cos^2 \theta = 1$

2. Show the equation for a cosine function with the exact same graph as $y = \sin x$.

3. Write the equation for a circle tangent to both axes, with its center in the third quadrant and an area equal to 100π square units.

4. Write the equation whose graph has the lines $x = 4$ and $x = -3$ as asymptotes.

5. Write the equation for a function symmetric with respect to the y-axis, having $(0, 1)$ as a maximum point, and asymptotic to the x-axis.

6. Write the polar coordinates represented by the complex number $-1 - i$.

7. Write an infinite geometric series having a limit of -1 for its sum.

8. Write the equations for two concentric circles with their centers at the origin, such that the area of the larger circle is twice that of the smaller.

COMPLETING THE CONNECTION
Identify the concept or relationship represented in the given illustration.

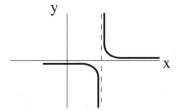

Introduction

In the *What Are You Likely to Be Asked* activity, students are expected to analyze given situations, reflecting on the mathematical concepts present. They then write one or more questions that are "likely to be asked" about that particular situation. To some extent, the objective of the activity for students is to make an association with certain typical situations and related questions that they have previously encountered. Encourage students to devise questions at a level of sophistication or maturity appropriate for their grade level.

Sample Exercises

Write one or more questions you are likely to be asked about the given situation.

1.
   - Find the area of the 60° sector.
   - Find the length of the arc associated with the 60° central angle.

NOTE: Students should be encouraged to come up with more than one question per exercise, if possible. Both suggested answers given here are appropriately difficult. Responses like the following, on the other hand, would be somewhat trivial:

- Find the length of the diameter.

- Find the area of the circle.

- Find the circumference of the circle.

The concepts treated by such questions are very basic; furthermore, they do not involve the 60° central angle. As needed, challenge students to avoid the overly simplistic response.

COMPLETING THE CONNECTION

Completing the Connection asks students to provide the information necessary to solve a given problem. For each problem situation, students should try to give several different sets of information that would be sufficient for solution. For example, on an "Elementary Algebra" page, students are asked to provide the information necessary to write an equation for a line. They might list the following:

- slope and intercept
- point on the line and slope
- *x*- and *y*-intercept
- two points on the line

For each exercise, write one or more questions that you are likely to be asked about the given situation.

	Given	What are you likely to be asked?
1.	The average of 5 scores is 83. Four of the scores are 78, 90, 66, and 84.	What is the fifth score?
2.	$P = 11x + 14$ triangle with sides $3x + 4$ and $2x + 9$	
3.	A line contains the points $(0, 0)$ and $(4, 7)$. The point $(5, 5)$ is not on the line.	
4.	The points $(0, 0)$, $(8, 0)$, and $(2, 5)$ are three vertices of a quadrilateral.	
5.	The length of a rectangle is 8 units more than the width. The area is 48 square units.	
6.	The sum of $100 is invested at an interest rate r. In two years the total grows to $140.00.	

COMPLETING THE CONNECTION

What information do you need to find the average of a set of four numbers?

For each exercise, write one or more questions that you are likely to be asked about the given situation.

Given	What are you likely to be asked?
1. $x^2y + xy^2$; $x = 4$, $y = -4$	Find the value of the expression.
2. (image: line segment from (3,4) to (11,8))	
3. (image: U-shaped figure with sides labeled d, d, d, $2d$, c)	
4. Six apples and three oranges cost $1.77. Two apples and five oranges cost $1.27.	
5. One endpoint of a line segment is $(0, 2)$ and the midpoint of the segment is $(-3, 5)$.	
6. $2x + 4y = 7$ $3x - 2y = 4$	

COMPLETING THE CONNECTION
What information do you need to write an equation for a line?

For each exercise, write one or more questions that you are likely to be asked about the given situation.

Given	What are you likely to be asked?
1. $x^2 + y^2 = 25$ $y = x^2$	What are the coordinates of the points of intersection?
2. The endpoints of the diameter of a circle are $(3, 5)$ and $(-2, 0)$.	
3. The line $2x + 3y = 7$ and the point $(1, 1)$.	
4. $f(x) = x^2 + 2$ and $g(x) = 2x + 5$	
5. $1, 3, 5, \ldots 39$	
6. The fourth term of an arithmetic sequence is 6; the seventh term of the same sequence is 12.	

COMPLETING THE CONNECTION

What information do you need to write the equation of a parabola?

For each exercise, write one or more questions that you are likely to be asked about the given situation.

Given	What are you likely to be asked?
1. One root of the equation $x^3 - 4x^2 + x - 4 = 0$ is i.	What are the other roots? What is the sum of the roots?
2. $7m + 6p + 7q = 0$ $2m + 2p + 3q = -1$ $8m + 3p + 5q = 3$	
3. $\log_b x = 2$ and $\log_b y = 3$.	
4. y varies directly as x, and $y_1 = 6$ when $x_1 = 5$, $x_2 = 15$.	
5. $(1, 7k), (-3, 5k)$ $m = -\dfrac{1}{2}$	
6. A rectangular garden is 12 meters wide and 18 meters long. It is surrounded by a walk of uniform width with an area of 70 square meters.	

COMPLETING THE CONNECTION
What information do you need to find the sum of an arithmetic series?

For each exercise, write one or more questions that you are likely to be asked about the given situation.

	Given	What are you likely to be asked?
1.	23° (isosceles triangle)	What is the measure of one of the base angles?
2.	A B D C; AC = 10, BD = 24	
3.	cubes labeled 1 and 3	
4.	regular octagon	
5.	circle with O, 4, 10	
6.	The distance between consecutive bases in major league baseball is 90 feet.	

COMPLETING THE CONNECTION
What information do you need to find the area of a 30°-60°-90° triangle?

For each exercise, write one or more questions that you are likely to be asked about the given situation.

Given	What are you likely to be asked?
1. $l \parallel m$ $3x + 20°$ → l $x + 90°$ → m	Given that the lines *l* and *m* are parallel, find the value of x.
2. $(3, 4), (5, 11), (10, k)$	
3. 10 / 45° / 45° / 20	
4. A convex polygon has 27 diagonals.	
5. A 7 10 B M C 12	
6. 4" 9"	

COMPLETING THE CONNECTION

What information do you need to find the area of a sector of a circle?

For each exercise, write one or more questions that you are likely to be asked about the given situation.

	Given	What are you likely to be asked?
1.	(right triangle with legs 3 and 4, hypotenuse 5)	What is the measure of each acute angle of the triangle?
2.	(isosceles triangle with 70° base angle, base 8 cm)	
3.	The line $2x + 3y = 9$ and the point P (4, 4).	
4.	$27 - 18 + 12 - 8 + \ldots$	
5.	The complex number $\sqrt{3 - i}$.	
6.	A flagpole casts a shadow 5 meters long. The angle of elevation of the sun is 50°.	

COMPLETING THE CONNECTION
What information do you need to find the sine of an angle of a right triangle?

For each exercise, write one or more questions that you are likely to be asked about the given situation.

Given	What are you likely to be asked?
1. Point P (2, 3) is on a circle with its center at the origin.	What is the equation for the circle?
2. A triangle has sides with lengths of 34, 23, and 42.	
3. Each leg of an isosceles triangle is 27 cm and each base angle measures 23°.	
4. $x^2 + y^2 + 6x - 2y - 15 = 0$ is the equation for a circle.	
5. One root of the equation $2x^3 - 5x^2 - 4x + 3 = 0$ is $x = 3$.	
6. A ball is dropped from a height of 14 meters. Each time the ball strikes the ground, it bounces back to a height that is three-fourths the distance from which it fell.	

COMPLETING THE CONNECTION

What information do you need to find the sum of an infinite geometric series that converges?

Introduction

The activities in *Making the Connection* offer a variety of non-routine problems based on concepts and relationships in algebra and geometry. There are two pages each of five different exercise formats (described below under "Sample Exercises"), plus two pages of "Geometry Through Algebraic Demonstration" that help students make key connections between geometry and algebra.

Sample Exercises

Department of Violations. In this activity, students analyze a given situation to determine where an error exists. They are asked to state the concept being "violated."

EXAMPLE: **Situation**　　　　　　**Violation**

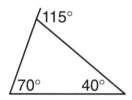

The measure of an exterior angle of a triangle must equal the sum of the remote interior angles.

Obvious Conclusion. In this activity, students are given a situation and certain additional information; they are asked to indicate an obvious conclusion that could be drawn.

EXAMPLE:
You are given the equation $3x + 4y = 12$ and the fact that $3(4) + 4(5) \neq 12$.

OBVIOUS CONCLUSION:
The point $(4, 5)$ is not on the line $3x + 4y = 12$.

Which One Doesn't Belong? In this activity, the students concentrate on critical attributes as they examine four given items and select one that doesn't belong with the others in the set. Their answers should state the common attribute of the three items that is missing from the fourth. Answers may vary.

EXAMPLE:

$x^2 - 4y^2$ $\qquad$ $x^2 - 9y^2$ $\qquad$ $\boxed{8x^2 - 49y^2}$ $\qquad$ $16x^2 - 25y^2$

ANSWER:

$8x^2 - 49y^2$ doesn't belong because the other three expressions represent differences of squares.

Tell All You Know. In this activity, students are expected to state all the mathematical "things" they know about a given situation. Answers will consist of lists that may refer to apparent relationships, properties, types of numbers used, and so forth.

EXAMPLE: ANSWERS:

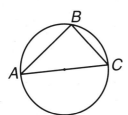

$\overline{AC}$ is the diameter.
$\angle ABC$ is an inscribed angle.
$\angle ABC$ is a right angle.
m $\angle ABC = 90°$.

Quantitative Comparison. In this activity, students compare two given quantities to decide whether one is greater than the other, whether they are equal, or whether the comparison cannot be determined from the given information. Emphasis is not on computation, but on thinking and reasoning.

EXAMPLE:

Write A if the first item is greater, B if the second item is greater, C if they are equal, D if there is not enough information to decide.

First item	Second item	Response
slope of line $y = 3x + 1$	slope of line $3x - y = 2$	C
volume of cylinder $h = 9$", $r = 2$"	volume of cylinder $h = 7$", $r = 3$"	B

For each of the five activity types described above, *Completing the Connection* asks students to create an original example similar to those presented on the page. These original examples should be shared through small-group or whole-class discussion.

The two pages at the conclusion of this section, called "Geometry Through Algebraic Demonstration," ask students to apply their algebraic skills to solve non-routine geometry problems.

In each of the following situations, find a mathematical concept that has been violated. Be prepared to discuss your response.

Situation	Violation
1. _trapezoid with top base x, side marked $(y-x)/2$, bottom base y_	The median of a trapezoid has a length equal to the average of the bases. Its length should be $\left(\dfrac{x+y}{2}\right)$.
2. $a - (b - 5) = a - b - 5$	
3. _triangle with sides 4.9 and 5.1_	
4. $(2, 5)\ (4, 3)\quad m = \dfrac{2 - 4}{5 - 3}$	
5. _circle of radius r with arc $\dfrac{\pi r}{4}$_	
6. $\dfrac{n^8}{n^2} = n^4$	
7. _angle diagram showing $85°$_	
8. $(x + 3)^2 = x^2 + 9$	

COMPLETING THE CONNECTION
Write another problem similar to the ones on this page.

In each of the following situations, find a mathematical concept that has been violated. Be prepared to discuss your response.

Situation	Violation
1. (right triangle with legs 5 and 8, hypotenuse 10)	$5^2 + 8^2 \neq 10^2$. In a right triangle, the lengths of the three sides must satisfy the Pythagorean Theorem.
2. $4(x + 3) = 4x + 3$	
3. (triangle with sides 3 and 4, angle 70°, base 5)	
4. $3^2 \cdot 3^5 = 9^7$	
5. (triangle with angles 115°, 70°, 40°)	
6. $\sqrt{12} = \sqrt{4(3)} = 4\sqrt{3}$	
7. (triangle with sides 5 and 5, angle 60°, base 4)	
8. $\dfrac{x + \cancel{4}}{\cancel{4}}$	

COMPLETING THE CONNECTION
Write another problem similar to the ones on this page.

What is the obvious conclusion for each of the following? Explain why your conclusion must be true.

1. Two solutions to the equation $x^2 - 7x + 12 = 0$ are $x = 3$ and $x = 4$. What can you conclude about the relationship between $x = -5$ and the given quadratic equation? *Since quadratic equations have exactly two roots $x = -5$ cannot be a solution to the given equation.*

2. A Pythagorean triple is 3, 4, 5. If two sides of a right triangle measure 30 and 40, what can you conclude is the measure of the third side?

3. The trinomial $x^2 - 4x + 2$ cannot be factored over the set of integers. As a result, what can you conclude about the solutions to the quadratic equation $x^2 - 4x + 2 = 0$?

4. Knowing that 7, 24, 25 is a Pythagorean triple, what can you conclude about 8, 24, 25?

5. This graph shows the parabola represented by the equation $y = ax^2 + bx + c$. What can you conclude about the solutions to the equation $ax^2 + bx + c = 0$?

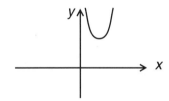

6. Knowing that the slope of the segment connecting points (0, 2) and (2, 8) is 3, what can you conclude about the slope of the segment connecting the points (0, 2) and (2, k), where $k > 8$?

COMPLETING THE CONNECTION
Write another problem similar to the ones on this page.

What is the obvious conclusion for each of the following? Explain why your conclusion must be true.

1. Consider the line for $3x + 4y = 24$ and the fact that $3(5) + 4(5) \neq 24$. What can you conclude as a result?

   The point (5, 5) is NOT on the line. If a point is on a line, the coordinates of the point must satisfy the equation for the line.

2. Lines *l* and *m* are cut by a transversal *t*. What can you conclude about *l* and *m*?

   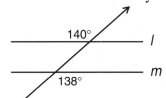

3. Point *A* is a solution to the inequality $y > x + 4$. What is the relationship between point *B* and the inequality $y < x + 4$?

   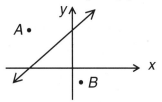

4. The length of each side of a pentagon is tripled. What can you conclude about the perimeter?

5. For the expression $x^2 + 2x - 8$, you get the value of 7 when $x = 3$ and the value of -5 when $x = 1$. What does this guarantee about a solution to $x^2 + 2x - 8 = 0$?

6. Two angles are supplementary and in the ratio of 1:1. What can you conclude as a result?

COMPLETING THE CONNECTION
Write another problem similar to the ones on this page.

Study the four items in each row, and circle the one that you feel does not belong with the others. Next to your answer, state the reason for your choice. Because there are different ways of looking at these items, answers may vary.

	A	B	C	D
1.	$35°, 65°$ (circled) The other pairs are complementary angles.	$40°, 50°$	$20°, 70°$	$45°, 45°$
2.	$\sqrt{12}$	$\sqrt{27}$	$\sqrt{24}$	$\sqrt{300}$
3.	$\dfrac{3a^2}{6a}$	$\dfrac{2a}{a^2}$	$\dfrac{a^2 + 2a}{2a + 4}$	$\dfrac{2ab}{4b}$
4.	3, 4, 5	5, 6, 7	5, 6, 12	4, 4, 4
5.	area of a square, $s = 4$	area of a rectangle, $l = 8, w = 4$	area of a triangle, $b = 8, h = 4$	area of a rhombus, $d_1 = 8, d_2 = 4$
6.	$y = x$ $y = x + 4$	$2x - y = 3$ $4x - 2y = 10$	$y = 4$ $y = 8$	$x + y = 4$ $x - y = 6$
7.	distance between $(0, 0)$ and $(5, 12)$	distance between $(0, 0)$ and $(-12, 5)$	distance between $(0, 0)$ and $(6, 6)$	distance between $(0, 0)$ and $(13, 0)$
8.	$\dfrac{9 - 6x}{6 - 9x}$	$\dfrac{x^2 - 4}{4 - x^2}$	$\dfrac{2x - 6}{6 - 2x}$	$\dfrac{x - a}{a - x}$

COMPLETING THE CONNECTION
Write another problem similar to the ones on this page.

Study the four items in each row, and circle the one that you feel does not belong with the others. Next to your answer, state the reason for your choice. Because there are different ways of looking at these items, answers may vary.

	A	B	C	D
1.	(S.S.A) The others are ways to show that two triangles are congruent.	S.S.S	S.A.S	A.S.A
2.	tangent	secant	chord	altitude
3.	$\sqrt{32}$	$\sqrt{98}$	$\sqrt{200}$	$\sqrt{22}$
4.	$y = 2x + 4$	$3y - 6x = 9$	$4y = 2x$	$-2x + y = -4$
5.	5, 12, 13	6, 8, 12	7, 24, 25	8, 15, 17
6.	$x^2 - 5x + 6$	$x^2 - x + 2$	$x^2 - 13x + 36$	$x^2 - 9x + 20$
7.	$1000°$	$540°$	$720°$	$360°$
8.	2^{-2}	$\left(\dfrac{1}{2}\right)^2$	$\sqrt{\dfrac{1}{16}}$	-2^2

COMPLETING THE CONNECTION
Write another problem similar to the ones on this page.

Study the given diagrams and expressions. List as many things as you can about each numbered item. Note that these are *not* problems to be solved; rather you are to list the characteristics and relationships you find in each situation.

1. 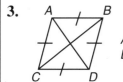	A line is shown.
	The slope of the line is positive.
	The y-intercept is $(0, b)$ with $b > 0$.
2. $2x^2 - 5x - 3 = 0$	
3. 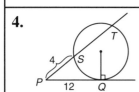 $AC = 6$ $BD = 8$	
4.	
5. Find the shaded area. m $\angle ABC = 40°$	
6. $\dfrac{x^2 + 9x}{x^2 - 9x}$	

COMPLETING THE CONNECTION
Write the expressions or draw the diagram for another problem
situation similar to the ones on this page.

Study the given diagrams and expressions. List as many things as you can about each numbered item. Note that these are *not* problems to be solved; rather you are to list the characteristics and relationships you find in each situation.

1. $l\|m$ 50° → l → m	Two parallel lines are cut by a transversal. All acute angles measure 50°. All obtuse angles measure 130°.
2. $3x - 6y = 12$ $x - 3y = 9$	
3. 130°	
4. B D 80° O 70° C A	
5.	
6. 8 cm 12 cm	

COMPLETING THE CONNECTION

Write the expressions or draw the diagram for another problem
situation similar to the ones on this page.

In each row, write A if the first item is greater, B if the second item is greater, C if they are equal, and D if there's not enough information to decide.

	First item	Second item	Response
1.	the average of the first 100 counting numbers.	50	A
2.	$(-2)^5$	2^{-5}	
3.	the measure of the exterior angle of a regular hexagon	the measure of the interior angle of an equilateral triangle	
4.	slope of $2x + 3y = 6$	slope of $4x - 6y = 12$	
5.	the measure of the arc with a central angle of 60°	the measure of the arc with an inscribed angle of 60°	
6.	the area of circle with radius 1	the area of a square with side π	
7.	the length of the diagonal of a unit square	the length of the diagonal of a unit cube	
8.	2^x	3^{2x}	

COMPLETING THE CONNECTION

Make up another problem similar to the ones on this page, comparing two related quantities.

In each row, write A if the first item is greater, B if the second item is greater, C if they are equal, and D if there's not enough information to decide.

	First item	Second item	Response
1.	the hypotenuse of a right triangle with legs 5, 12	the side of a rhombus with a diagonals 10, 24	C
2.	$|-5|$	opposite of the opposite of -5	
3.	$\dfrac{x-a}{a-x}$ $x \neq a$	1	
4.	area of $\triangle DEC$	area of $\triangle AFD$	
5.	$(x+1)^3$	$x^3 + 1$	
6.	the area of the sector	area of the sector	
7.	$\dfrac{a^2b}{a}$; $a = -\dfrac{1}{4}$, $b = 2\dfrac{1}{2}$	$\dfrac{-a^3b}{a^2}$; $a = -\dfrac{1}{4}$, $b = 2\dfrac{1}{2}$	
8.	area of an equilateral triangle with side 10	area of a 6-8-10 right triangle	

COMPLETING THE CONNECTION
Make up another problem similar to the ones on this page, comparing two related quantities.

The following geometry problems can be solved with algebraic concepts and skills. For each problem, write an algebraic demonstration to answer the question posed. The first one is done as an example.

1. Show an algebraic demonstration to confirm that the only consecutive integers that can represent the lengths of the sides of a right triangle are 3, 4, 5.

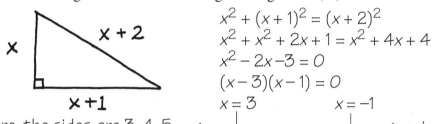

$$x^2 + (x + 1)^2 = (x + 2)^2$$
$$x^2 + x^2 + 2x + 1 = x^2 + 4x + 4$$
$$x^2 - 2x - 3 = 0$$
$$(x - 3)(x - 1) = 0$$
$$x = 3 \qquad x = -1$$

Therefore, the sides are 3, 4, 5. ⟵⏋
No other consecutive integers would work. ⟶ reject

2. One dimension of a rectangle is increased 10% and the other is decreased 10%. What happens to the area of the rectangle? What happens to the area if the dimensions change by 50% instead of 10%? What happens to the area if the dimensions change by 99% instead of 10%?

3. Two vertices of a triangle are (0, 0) and (3, 4). If the third vertex is $(k, 0)$, find the value(s) of k such that the area of the triangle is 20 square units.

4. Show the connection between the terms of the expansion of the binomial $(a + b)^3$ and the volume of rectangular solids. Before you combine the like terms, how many rectangular solids would exist?

The following geometry problems can be solved with algebraic concepts and skills. For each problem, write an algebraic demonstration to answer the question posed. The first one is done as an example.

1. A square is cut into two rectangles. Can the larger rectangle have twice the area of the smaller one? Can it have twice the perimeter? What ratio satisfies each condition described?

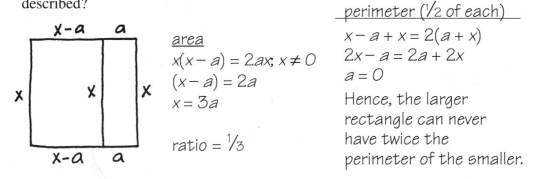

area
$$x(x - a) = 2ax; x \neq 0$$
$$(x - a) = 2a$$
$$x = 3a$$

ratio = $\frac{1}{3}$

perimeter ($\frac{1}{2}$ of each)
$$x - a + x = 2(a + x)$$
$$2x - a = 2a + 2x$$
$$a = 0$$

Hence, the larger rectangle can never have twice the perimeter of the smaller.

2. Demonstrate what happens to the volume of a cylinder when the radius of the base is tripled and the height is cut in half.

3. For a general equilateral triangle, discuss the placement of line segment *XY* such that the area of the small equilateral triangle is half the area of the large equilateral triangle.

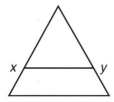

4. Suppose the corners of a 2-inch square are cut off to form a regular octagon. How far from the corner of the square must each cut start?

NOTE: All answers provided here are suggestions. Other answers are possible.

Section 1: How Do You Know That?

Page 2 (Elementary Algebra/1)

2. Since 10 is the greatest common factor of 30, 20, and 50, the greatest common factor could not be $5x$. **3.** The product of any two negative numbers is positive. Multiplying this product by another negative number would give a negative final product. **4.** In $y = 1/2x + 2$, the slope is $+1/2$, and therefore the line would rise from left to right. **5.** $(x + y)^2 = x^2 + 2xy + y^2$, and since the numerator is not the same as the denominator, the fraction would not simplify to 1. *Note:* If either x or y, but not both, is 0, the fraction would reduce to 1. **6.** m^2 would be non-negative for any real number m. **7.** To find the y-intercept, you can allow x to equal 0. Doing this gives $-4y = 8$ and $y = -2$. **8.** $(x + 3)^2$ would give $x^2 + 6x + 9$; hence, $x^2 + 9$ is not factorable. (The difference of two squares would be factorable.)

Page 3 (Elementary Algebra/2)

2. 4 is not a factor of 30. **3.** $x - a$ and $a - x$ are opposites. As a result, the fraction would reduce to -1. For example: $\dfrac{7-4}{4-7} = \dfrac{3}{-3} = -1$ **4.** $(a + b)^2$ requires a product of three terms: $a^2 + 2ab + b^2$. **5.** If you divide $2x^2 - 17x + 8$ by $2x - 1$, you get $x - 9$. Therefore, $2x - 1$ is a factor of the trinomial. **6.** If 7 is substituted for x, each factor $(x - 4)$, $(x - 5)$, and $(x - 6)$ is non-zero;

therefore, the product cannot be 0. **7.** The lines are different and each line has a slope of 3. Lines with the same slope are parallel. **8.** The slope of the line segment joining pairs of points is the same.

$$\frac{7-(-8)}{4-(-1)} = \frac{15}{3} = 3; \frac{7-(-5)}{4-0} = \frac{12}{4} = 3$$

Thus the three points are collinear.

Page 4 (Intermediate Algebra/1)

2. You get the same value for y if you use x or $-x$. **3.** In $y = mx + b$ form, the equations are $y = 2/3\, x - 2$ and $y = 2/3\, x - 3/2$. Since the slopes are the same, the equations represent parallel lines. **4.** In order to have rational roots, the $\sqrt{8}$ would have to be a rational number. $\sqrt{8} = 2\sqrt{2}$, which is irrational. **5.** When you divide the polynomial by $x - 2$, you get a remainder of 4. Therefore $x - 2$ is not a factor. **6.** In the equation for a circle, the coefficients of the x^2 and y^2 terms must be the same. **7.** $\dfrac{48}{24}, \dfrac{24}{12}$, and $\dfrac{12}{6}$ produce a common ratio, which is the requirement for a geometric sequence. **8.** Let $\log_b x = c$ and $\log_b y = d$. Then $\log_b x + \log_b y = c + d$. $b^c = x$ and $b^d = y$. Therefore, $b^c b^d = xy$; $b^{c+d} = xy$. $\log_b xy = c + d$

Page 5 (Intermediate Algebra/2)

2. $(a + bi)(a - bi) = a^2 - b^2i^2 = a^2 - b^2(-1) = a^2 + b^2$, which is a real number. **3.** $y = x^2 - 4x + 4$ can be written as $y = (x - 2)^2$, and $y = (x - 2)^2$ is a translation of $y = x$, two units to the right. **4.** Since $x^2 - 4y^2 - 6x = 7$ can be written $(x^2 - 6x + 9) - 4y^2 = 16$,

$\dfrac{(x-3)^2}{4} - y^2 = 4$. The equation represents a hyperbola with center (3, 0). **5.** Since 4 raised to a positive integer power results in a number that ends in either a 4 or a 6, you cannot obtain 25 by raising 4 to a positive integer power. With $4^2 = 16$ and $4^3 = 64$, the value of x would be between 2 and 3 to have $4^x = 25$. **6.** The function is increasing because the value of the function increases as x increases. **7.** If 2/3 is substituted for x, the value of the equation is not 0. **8.** The functions are inverses because each does the inverse mapping of the other. $f(1) = 4$ while $g(4) = 1$; f maps 1 to 4, while g maps 4 to 1.

Page 6 (Geometry/1)

2. $5^2 + 6^2 = 25 + 36 = 51 \neq 7^2$
3. $10 + 10 < 25$. In any triangle, the sum of the lengths of two sides must be greater than the length of the third side. **4.** With Angle-Angle-Angle, the two triangles would have the same shape. Without any information about the sides, you could not guarantee congruence. **5.** An inscribed angle would have a measure of 1/2 the degree measure of the intercepted arc. Since a semicircle gives 180°, the angle measure would be 90° and the triangle would be a right triangle. **6.** Congruent chords are equidistant from the center of the circle. Therefore, the midpoints are all the same distance from the center, and this defines another circle. **7.** For a regular polygon, the measure of the interior angle is $\dfrac{(n-2)\,180}{n}$. The measure of each exterior angle is defined as 360/n. If the interior and exterior angles are congruent, then $\dfrac{(n-2)\,180}{n} = \dfrac{360}{n}$. Since $n \neq 0$, $(n-2)(180) = 360$, $n - 2 = 2$, $n = 4$. Therefore, the polygon is a square. **8.** The formula for the sum of

the measures of the interior angles is $(n-2)180°$. Hence, the sum must be a multiple of 180°, and 1900° is not a multiple of 180°.

Page 7 (Geometry/2)

2. Since all angles are right angles and the sides are in proportion, all squares must be similar to one another. **3.** Each exterior angle at the base is supplementary to the adjacent base angle. With the base angles of the isosceles triangle being congruent, the exterior angles are congruent, because supplements of congruent angles are congruent. **4.** $5^2 + 6^2 = 25 + 36 = 61 < 10^2$. For a triangle to be obtuse, $a^2 + b^2 < c^2$, where c is the longest side. **5.** Both pairs of opposite sides must be congruent to have a parallelogram. The horizontal sides have lengths that are not the same (8 units and 11 units). **6.** The slopes of the lines through any two of the points are equal. Hence the points lie on the same line and are collinear. **7.** In any non-square rectangle, the diagonals intersect to form acute and obtuse angles. Since right angles are not formed, the diagonals would not be perpendicular. **8.** Since the two lines are parallel, a pair of interior angles on the same side of the transversal would be supplementary. In the triangle formed by the bisectors and the transversal, the two halves of the interior angles would be complementary, and the angle formed by the bisectors would be a right angle.

Page 8 (Pre-calculus/1)

2. The period of $y = 2 \cos x$ is 2π. For $y = 2 \cos kx$, the period is $\dfrac{2\pi}{k}$.

3. 330° is an angle in the fourth quadrant with 30° as a reference angle; sin 330° $= -\sin 30° = -0.5$ **4.** $2 \sin x \cos x = \sin 2x$. Since the maximum value for $y = \sin x$ is 1, the maximum value for 2 (2 sin x cos x) would be 2. **5.** Because complex

roots must occur in conjugate pairs.
6. Vertical asymptotes occur where y is undefined. With $x^2 - 36$ in the denominator, $x = \pm 6$ would make the denominator 0. **7.** $\log_2 16 = 4$ and $\log_2 32 = 5$ **8.** $x^2 + y^2 = 2$ has radius $\sqrt{2}$ and area $= 2\pi$. $x^2 + y^2 = 1$ has radius 1 and area $= \pi$.

Page 9 (Pre-calculus/2)

2. $\sin x = \sin(2k\pi + x)$ where $k = 1, 2, 3, \dots$ **3.** Sine function increases from $0°$ to $90°$ and 1 radian $\approx 57°$. **4.** Because you cannot find a common difference or common ratio. **5.** The first series is an infinite geometric series with $r = 1/2$. The second series is not an infinite geometric series. The second series can be represented as: $1/2 + \underline{1/3 + 1/4} + \underline{1/5 + 1/6 + 1/7 + 1/8} + 1/9 \dots$ which is greater than $1/2 + \underline{1/4 + 1/4} + \underline{1/8 + 1/8 + 1/8 + 1/8} + \dots$ which equals $1/2 + 1/2 + 1/2 + \dots$ Continuing, you get an infinite number of 1/2's; therefore the series diverges. **6.** If $2 - i$ is a root, $2 + i$ must also be a root. **7.** The appropriate row of Pascal's Triangle, 1 5 10 10 5 1, has a sum of 2^5 or 32. **8.** Law of Cosines:
$c^2 = a^2 + b^2 - 2ab \cos C$. If C is a right angle, you get:
$c^2 = a^2 + b^2 - 2ab \cos 90°$
$c^2 = a^2 + b^2 - 2ab(0)$
$c^2 = a^2 + b^2$

Section 2: Sometimes

Page 12 (Elementary Algebra/1)

2. *True:* $2^2 = 2(2)$; *False:* $1^2 = 2(1)$
3. *True:* $2(2) < 3(2)$; *False:* $2(-2) < 2(-3)$
4. *True:* $k = 8$; *False:* $k = 4$
5. *True:* $(0 + 1)^2 = 0^2 + 1^2$; *False:* $(1 + 2)^2 = 1^2 + 2^2$
6. *True:* $k = -1$; *False:* $k = 10$

7. *True:* $\sqrt{4} < \sqrt{4^3}$,

False: $\sqrt{\dfrac{1}{4}} < \sqrt{\left(\dfrac{1}{4}\right)^3}$

8. *True:* $3(4/3) > 3$; *False:* $3(3/4) > 3$

Page 13 (Elementary Algebra/2)

2. *True:* $1^2 = 1^2$; *False:* $(-1)^2 = (1)^2$
3. *True:* $x = 2$; *False:* $x = 1/2$
4. *True:* $4^2 = 2^4$; *False:* $3^2 = 2^3$
5. *True:* $\sqrt{0 + 4} = \sqrt{0} + \sqrt{4}$
False: $\sqrt{9 + 4} = \sqrt{9} + \sqrt{4}$
6. *True:* $4x^2 + 12x + 9$;
False: $4x^2 + 10x + 9$
7. *True:* $y = 3x + 6$; *False:* $y = 3x - 6$
8. *True:* $(8, 4),(6, 3)$; *False:* $(1, 3),(2, 5)$

Page 14 (Intermediate Algebra/1)

2. *True:* $\sqrt{4}$; *False:* $\sqrt{-9}$
3. *True:* $(5, 0)$; *False:* $(5, 2)$
4. *True:* $(1 + 2i)(1 - 2i) = 1 + 4 = 5$;
False: $(1 + 2i)(1 - 3i) = 7 - i$
5. *True:* $x = 5$; *False:* $x = 10$
6. *True:* $y = 2x + 3$ and $y = 2x + 4$;
False: $y = 2x + 3$ and $2y - 4x = 6$
7. *True:* $y = x$; *False:* $x = 3$
8. *True:* $f(x) = 2x - 3$, $g(x) = (x + 3)/2$;
False: $f(x) = -x + 3$; $g(x) = -x - 3$

Page 15 (Intermediate Algebra/2)

2. *True:* $\sqrt{2} + \sqrt{8}$; *False:* $\sqrt{2} + -\sqrt{2}$
3. *True:* $y = x$ and $y = -x$;
False: $x = 3$ and $y = 3$
4. *True:* $\sqrt[3]{-27}$; *False:* $\sqrt{-27}$
5. *True:* $x^2 - 4y^2 = 36$; *False:* $xy = 4$
6. *True:* k is even; *False:* k is odd
7. *True:* $y = 1/2\, x + 1$; *False:* $y = x^2$
8. *True:* $(5 + 0)^3$; *False:* $(5 + 3)^3$

Page 16 (Geometry/1)

2. *True:*   *False:*

3. *True:*   *False:*

4. *True:*   *False:*

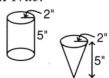 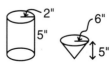

5. *True:*   *False:*

6. *True:*
if original circle
has radius <4   *False:*
if original circle
has radius >4

7. *True:*   *False:*

8. *True:*   *False:*

Page 17(Geometry/2)

2. *True:*   *False:*

3. *True:*   *False:*

4. *True:*
SQUARE   *False:*
RECTANGLE

5. *True:*
RHOMBUS   *False:*
PARALLELOGRAM

6. *True:*
$120°/60°$ *False:*
$120°$ $60°$

7. *True:* reflection; *False:* dilation
8. *True:*   *False:*

Page 18 (Pre-calculus/1)
 2. *True:* $k = 9$; *False:* $k = -9$ **3.** *True:*
$x^3 - x^2 - 4x + 4 = 0$; *False:* $x^3 - 8 = 0$
 4. *True:* $y = |x|$; *False:* $y = |x - 5|$
 5. *True:* $r = 10$; *False:* $r = 3$

 6. *True:* $a = 2, r = \dfrac{1}{2}$; *False:* $a = 2, r = 3$

7. *True:* $r = 3, f(x) = (x - 1)^3$;
False: $r = 2, f(x) = (x - 1)^2$
8. *True:* $f(x) = x^3$; *False:* $f(x) = |x|$

Page 19 (Pre-calculus/2)
 2. *True:* $x^4 - 5x^2 + 4 = 0$;
False: $x^4 - 3x^2 - 4 = 0$
 3. *True:* $k = 4$; *False:* $k = 3$
 4. *True:* $a = 0°, b = 45°$;
False: $a = 30°, b = 60°$
 5. *True:* $r = 3, y = x^3$;
False: $r = 2, y = x^2$
 6. *True:* $\log_2 32$; *False:* $\log_2 10$
 7. *True:* $y = 3$; *False:* $y = 5^2$
 8. *True:* $x^4 - 5x^2 + 4 = 0$;
False: $x^4 + 10x^2 + 9 = 0$

Section 3: What If?

Page 22 (Elementary Algebra/1)
 2. The point (6, 4) is not on the line.
 3. The graph is translated up on the y-axis. **4.** The slope of the line will be positive. **5.** The lines in the graph are perpendicular. **6.** The value of the expression is less than 0. **7.** The point is translated right 2 units and up 2 units.
 8. The expression is a difference of two perfect squares.

Page 23 (Elementary Algebra/2)
 2. The inequality is reversed; that is, $-x > -2$. **3.** The absolute value remains the same. **4.** Since $\sqrt{2x} = \sqrt{2}\sqrt{x}$, the value will be r(2) times greater. **5.** The denominator equals 0 and the fraction is not defined. **6.** The integers remain consecutive and are defined by $2x, 2x + 2, 2x + 4$. **7.** The slope of the line will be doubled. **8.** The lines are parallel and there is no point of intersection. The solution is the empty set.

Page 24 (Intermediate Algebra/1)
 2. $i^n = -1$ if n is even. **3.** The point (0, 3) is inside the circle. **4.** The roots are real. **5.** The parabola flattens as x increases. **6.** The sum converges to a limit. **7.** Then x varies jointly as w and z

and inversely as the square of y. **8.** For $b = 2$, the line intersects the hyperbola at $(1, 1)$, and for $b = -2$, the line intersects the hyperbola at $(-1, -1)$.

Page 25 (Intermediate Algebra/2)

2. The quadrilateral formed is a rhombus. **3.** The parabola has a maximum point. The graph will be concave, opening downward. **4.** The roots are complex. **5.** The sum diverges. **6.** The sum is doubled. **7.** It is divided by $\sqrt{2}$. **8.** The function and the inverse function are the same.

Page 26 (Geometry/1)

2. The slope is doubled. **3.** The distance is unchanged. **4.** A circle concentric to the original circle is formed. **5.** The area increases as the length changes from 4 to 9. The area goes from 8 to 18, an increase of 2-1/4 times. **6.** The length of the median is doubled. **7.** The arc will be cut in half. **8.** The volume will be 8 times greater.

Page 27 (Geometry/2)

2. The area stays the same. **3.** The length of the hypotenuse will double. **4.** The length of each side of the larger is increased by 10. **5.** The area of the sector will be 8 times greater. **6.** The volume will be 27 times greater. **7.** The figure formed will be a rhombus. **8.** The sum of the measures will increase 720°.

Page 28 (Pre-calculus/1)

2. You get another geometric sequence. **3.** The equation becomes $(x - 8)^2 + y^2 = 9$. **4.** You get two hyperbolas instead of one: $xy = 1$ and $xy = -1$; therefore, you have a branch in each quadrant. **5.** The area gets larger. **6.** The symmetry changes—from a graph that is symmetric about the y-axis to a graph that is symmetric about the origin. **7.** The hyperbola becomes asymptotic to $y = \pm x$. **8.** You get a rose with n petals.

Page 29 (Pre-calculus/2)

2. The graph is stretched out. **3.** The series converges to a limit. **4.** You get another arithmetic sequence with the same common difference as the original sequence. **5.** The graph has any portion below the x-axis reflected over the x-axis. **6.** The function is periodic. **7.** The sum gets squared. **8.** The population is almost doubled, to 77,948.

Section 4: Example to Fit the Condition

Page 32 (Elementary Algebra/1)

2. $(0, 10)$, $(10, 0)$, $(-10, 0)$, $(0, -10)$ **3.** $(6xy^3)(-3x^2y)$ **4.** $2x^2 - 5x - 12$ **5.** $x^2 - x - 6 = 0$ **6.** $4x^2 + 12x + 9 = 0$

7. $y = -x + 2$, $y = x$ **8.** $\dfrac{x^2 + 9}{x + 3}$

CTC. The difference of two squares.

Page 33 (Elementary Algebra/2)

2. $b^3 \div b^2$ **3.** $(0, 0)$, $(6, -4)$, $(-6, 4)$
4.

5. $\sqrt{2}, \sqrt{3}, \sqrt{7}$ **6.** $x^3 + 5x^2 + 6x = 0$
7. $(x + y)^2 = x^2 + 2xy + y^2$ **8.** $1.1b$
CTC. Lines with the same slope are parallel.

Page 34 (Intermediate Algebra/1)

2. $x^2 + y^2 = 49$, $(x - 4)^2 + y^2 = 9$; $(x - 10)^2 + y^2 = 9$; $(x^2 - 14) + y^2 = 49$
3. $x^2 - 2x + 2 = 0$ **4.** 2, 4, 6, 8, 10
5. $(2x + y)^3$ **6.** $f(x) = -1/2\,x + 4$; $f^{-1}(x) = -2x + 8$ **7.** $(-4, 0)$, $(4, 0)$, $\left(0, 4\sqrt{3}\right)$ **8.** The speed for flying a fixed distance is inversely proportional to the flight time.
CTC. The circle with equation $x^2 + y^2 = 16$

Page 35 (Intermediate Algebra/2)

2. $x^2 + y^2 = 25$; $y = 5$ **3.** $x^2 + y^2 = 25$; $y = x^2 - 5$ **4.** $2^4 = 4^2$ **5.** $|2x - 1| \le 7$
6. 18, 13, 8, 3, -2, -7 **7.** $x^3 + x^2 + 25x + 25 = 0$ **8.** $C = 2\pi r$
CTC. The slope of a line.

Page 36 (Geometry/1)
  2. Square **3.** Square

  4.

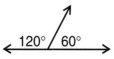

  5. Base: $l = 4$, $w = 3$; $h = 3$;
  Base: $l = 6$, $w = 3$; $h = 2$
  6.

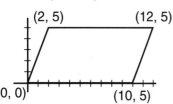

  (2, 5)   (12, 5)
  (0, 0)   (10, 5)

  7. **8.**

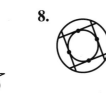

CTC. The measure of an inscribed angle is one-half the measure of the intercepted arc.

Page 37 (Geometry/2)
  2.

  3.

  4.

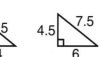

  3   5
    4
  4.5   7.5
      6

  5. **6.**

  60°

  7. **8.**

CTC. Congruent triangles using SAS.

Page 38 (Pre-calculus/1)
  2.

  3. $(x - 3)^2 + (y - 3)^2 = 9$ **4.** 210°, 225°, 240° **5.** area = 1/2 ab sin C (for a triangle with sides a, b, c) **6.** $(\sqrt{2}, 45)$

  7. $\dfrac{(x + 5)^2}{25} + \dfrac{(y + 6)^2}{36} = 1$

  8. $1 + 1/2 + 1/4 + 1/8 + \ldots$
  CTC. The sine curve and the cosine curve are out of phase by 90°.

Page 39 (Pre-calculus/2)
  2. $y = \cos(90° - x)$ **3.** $(x + 10)^2 + (y + 10)^2 = 100$ **4.** $y = \dfrac{1}{(x + 3)(x - 4)}$

  5. $y = \dfrac{1}{2^{|x|}}$ **6.** $(\sqrt{2}, 225°)$

  7. $-1/2 - 1/4 - 1/8 - 1/16 - \ldots$
  8. $x^2 + y^2 = 9$ and $x^2 + y^2 = 18$
  CTC. Horizontal and vertical asymptotes.

Section 5: What Are You Likely to Be Asked?

Page 42 (Elementary Algebra/1)
  2. What is the expression for the missing side? **3.** What is the equation of the line passing through (5, 5) that is parallel to the line containing the other two points? **4.** What are the coordinates of the fourth point so that the quadrilateral is a parallelogram? **5.** What is the perimeter of the figure? **6.** What is the rate of interest?
  CTC. (a) the individual numbers, (b) the sum of the four numbers.

Page 43 (Elementary Algebra/2)
  2. What is the equation for the line? **3.** What is an expression for the area of the figure? **4.** What is the cost of one apple? **5.** What are the coordinates of the other endpoint of the segment? **6.** What is the ordered pair that satisfies the system of equations?

CTC. (a) slope and intercept, (b) *x* and *y* intercepts, (c) slope and a point on the line, (d) two points on the line.

Page 44 (Intermediate Algebra/1)
2. What is the equation for the circle?
3. What is the equation for the line passing through the point (1, 1) that is perpendicular to the given line? **4.** What is the value of $f(g(5))$? **5.** How many terms are in the sequence? **6.** What is the first term of the sequence?
CTC. (a) the coordinates of the vertex and the value of "a" in $y = a(x - h)^2 + k$, (b) the coordinates of the focus and the equation of the directrix, (c) the coordinates of three points on the parabola, (d) the coordinates of the vertex and the focus.

Page 45 (Intermediate Algebra/2)
2. What are the coordinates for the ordered triple that satisfies the system of equations? **3.** What is the $\log_b xy$?
4. What is the value of y_2? **5.** What is the value of *k* that will result in the given ordered pairs being on the line with slope –1/2? **6.** What is the area of the garden and walk together?
CTC. (a) the value of the first term, the common difference, and the number of terms, (b) the value of the first term, last term, and the number of terms.

Page 46 (Geometry/1)
2. What is the area of the rhombus?
3. What is the ratio of the volumes?
4. What is the measure of each interior angle? **5.** How long is chord $\overline{AB}$?
6. What is the shortest distance from home plate to second base?
CTC. (a) the length of any one side, (b) base and height (for example, the length of the hypotenuse and the length of the altitude to the hypotenuse).

Page 47 (Geometry/2)
2. What is the value of *k* so that the three points are collinear? **3.** What is the perimeter of the isosceles trapezoid?

4. How many sides does the polygon have? **5.** What is the length of $\overline{BM}$ and $\overline{CM}$? **6.** What is the volume of the cone?
CTC. (a) the length of the radius and the measure of the central angle, (b) the area of the full circle and the measure of the central angle.

Page 48 (Pre-calculus/1)
2. What is the perimeter of the triangle?
3. What is the distance from *P* to the given line? **4.** What is the sum of the infinite series? **5.** What is the number expressed in polar form? **6.** What is the height of the flagpole?
CTC. the length of the hypotenuse and the side opposite the given angle.

Page 49 (Pre-calculus/2)
2. What is the measure of the largest angle? **3.** What is the length of the altitude to the base? **4.** What are the coordinates of the center? **5.** What is the sum of the other two roots? **6.** What is the total distance the ball travels before stopping?
CTC. (a) the first term and the common ratio, (b) the first two terms.

Section 6: Making the Connection

Page 53 (Department of Violations/1)
2. Distributive Property
3. Corresponding parts of congruent triangles must be congruent.
4. Definition of slope **5.** Formula for circumference **6.** Law of Division of Exponential Expressions **7.** The two angles must add to half of 180°.
8. Squaring a binomial produces a trinomial.

Page 54 (Department of Violations/2)
2. Distributive Property **3.** Sides of 3, 4, and 5 indicate that the triangle is a right triangle with the longest side opposite the 90° angle. **4.** In $x^a x^b$, you add the exponents but keep the base. **5.** The exterior angle of a triangle has a

71

measure equal to the sum of the two remote interior angles. **6.** The $\sqrt{4}$ was not taken in the simplication of the product. **7.** An isosceles triangle with a 60° vertex angle must be equilateral. **8.** Only factors may be cancelled.

Page 55 (Obvious Conclusion/1)
2. The hypotenuse must be 50 because 30, 40, 50 is a multiple of 3, 4, 5. **3.** Since the equation cannot be written in the form $(x + a)(x + b) = 0$, the roots of the equation are not rational. **4.** 8, 24, 25 is not a Pythagorean triple since 7, 24, 25 is. **5.** The solutions are complex. If the solutions were real, the parabola would intersect the x-axis. **6.** The slope is greater than 3.

Page 56 (Obvious Conclusion/2)
2. Alternate exterior angles are not congruent, so lines l and m are not parallel. **3.** B is a solution to $y < x + 4$, since B is below the line. **4.** The perimeter is tripled, because when you multiply each of the addends by 3, the sum is also multiplied by 3. **5.** The solution is between 1 and 3; since the function values change sign between 1 and 3, there is a place between 1 and 3 where the function value must be 0. **6.** The angles are right angles. Congruent supplementary angles measure 90° each.

Page 57 (Which One Doesn't Belong?/1)
2. C; the others simplify to a number times $\sqrt{3}$. **3.** B; the others reduce to a/2. **4.** C; the others are sets that could be sides of a triangle. **5.** B; the others have areas equal to 16. **6.** D; the other lines are parallel. **7.** C; the other distances are each 13. **8.** A; the other expressions equal –1.

Page 58 (Which One Doesn't Belong?/2)
2. D; the others are lines or segments in a circle. **3.** D; the others simplify to a

number times $\sqrt{2}$. **4.** C; the others have a slope of 2. **5.** B; the others are Pythagorean triples. **6.** B; the others are factorable over the set of integers. **7.** A; the others represent sums of the measures of interior angles of polygons. **8.** D; the others equal 1/4.

Page 59 (Tell All You Know/1)
2. Quadratic equation; equation has two roots; the sum of the roots is 5/2. **3.** Area is 24 square units; the figure is a rhombus; the diagonals are perpendicular. **4.** $\overleftrightarrow{PQ}$ is tangent to the circle, o(PT)is a secant to the circle; $(PQ)^2 = (PT)(PS)$. **5.** Radius is 6 inches; central angle measures 40°; the sector is 1/9 of the area of the circle; the length $\overset{\frown}{AC}$ is $\pi d/_9$. **6.** The fraction is not equal to 1; $x \neq 0$ or 9; the numerator and denominator are factorable.

Page 60 (Tell All You Know/2)
2. The lines intersect; the slope of one line is 1/2 and the slope of the other is 1/3; to solve the system, double both sides of the second equation and subtract. **3.** The triangle is isosceles; the interior base angles measure 50°; the base angles are congruent; the sum of the remote interior angles is 130°. **4.** $\overline{AB} \parallel \overline{DC}$; $m\angle DCO = 70°$; $m\angle OBA = 80°$; $\triangle DOC \sim \triangle BOA$. **5.** The slope of the line is negative; the line passes through the origin; points in the shaded region satisfy the inequality $y > kx$; the points on the line are not part of the solution. **6.** The figure is a cylinder; the radius of the base is 4 cm; $V = \pi r^2 h$.

Page 61 (Quantitative Comparison/1)
2. B **3.** C **4.** B **5.** B **6.** B **7.** B **8.** D

Page 62 (Quantitative Comparison/2)
2. A **3.** B **4.** C **5.** D **6.** A **7.** B **8.** A

Page 63 (Geometry Through Algebraic Demonstration/1)
2. For changes of 10%: original A = ab;

new A = (1.1a)(0.9b) = 0.99ab; decrease in area of 1%. For changes of 50%: original A = ab; new A = (1.5a)(0.5b) = 0.75ab; decrease in area of 25%. For changes of 99% : original A = ab; new A = (1.99a)(0.01b) = 0.0199ab; decrease in area of approximately 98%.

3.

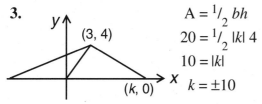

$A = \frac{1}{2}bh$

$20 = \frac{1}{2}|k|\,4$

$10 = |k|$

$k = \pm 10$

Note: Absolute value helps generate the two solutions to the problem.

4. $(a + b)^3 = a^3 + 3a^2b + 3ab^2 + b^3$; a^3: a cube with an edge of a; $3a^2b$: three rectangular solids, each a by a by b; $3ab^2$: three rectangular solids, each a by b by b; b^3: a cube with an edge of b. Thus there would be eight solids before you combine like terms.

Page 64 (Geometry Through Algebraic Demonstration/2)

2. Original: $V = \pi r^2 h$
New: $V = \pi(3r)^2\, 1/2h$
$= 9/2\, \pi r^2 h$

The new volume is 4.5 times the original volume.

3.   Original: $A_1 = \frac{s^2}{4}\sqrt{3}$

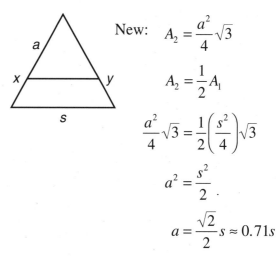

New: $A_2 = \frac{a^2}{4}\sqrt{3}$

$A_2 = \frac{1}{2}A_1$

$\frac{a^2}{4}\sqrt{3} = \frac{1}{2}\left(\frac{s^2}{4}\right)\sqrt{3}$

$a^2 = \frac{s^2}{2}$.

$a = \frac{\sqrt{2}}{2}s \approx 0.71s$

Therefore, $\overline{XY}$ should be placed 71% of the way from the vertex to the opposite side. ($\overline{XY}$ must be parallel to the base.)

4. $2 - 2x = x\sqrt{2}$

$2 = 2x + x\sqrt{2}$

$2 = x(2 + \sqrt{2})$

$x = \dfrac{2}{2 + \sqrt{2}}$

$x \approx 0.59$

Therefore, the cut is made at approximately 0.59 inch from each vertex of the square.